Alfred's

MEZZO/ALTO VOLUME 2

Singer's Library of Musical Theatre

32 SONGS FROM STAGE & FILM

A treasury of songs from stage and film in their original keys, selected by vocal range. Authentic arrangements transcribed from original vocal scores, with authoritative historical and contextual commentary, audition tips, and 16-bar cut suggestions.

EDITED AND COMPILED BY
JOHN L. HAAG AND JEREMY MANN

INTRODUCTION BY BARBARA IRVINE

Alfred Publishing Co., Inc.
16320 Roscoe Blvd., Suite 100
P.O. Box 10003
Van Nuys, CA 91410-0003
alfred.com

ISBN-10: 0-7390-4969-0
ISBN-13: 978-0-7390-4969-3

Cover Photos
Curtains: © iStockphoto.com / tobkatrina • Manhattan skyline: © iStockphoto.com / BRANDONJ74

Contents

Song Title	Show	Page	Vocal Range
Back on Base	*Closer Than Ever*	.29	
Holding to the Ground	*Falsettos*	.65	
How Can I Wait?	*Paint Your Wagon*	169	
I Know the Truth	*Elton John and Tim Rice's "Aida"*	.60	
If You Hadn't but You Did	*Two on the Aisle*	202	
It's a Fine Life	*Oliver!*	161	
Ladies	*Destry Rides Again*	.56	
Last Midnight	*Into The Woods*	107	
Lazy Afternoon	*The Golden Apple*	.85	
Like It Was	*Merrily We Roll Along*	140	
A Little Brains, A Little Talent	*Damn Yankees*	.34	
A Little Girl From Little Rock	*Gentlemen Prefer Blondes*	.79	
Mad About the Boy	*Oh! Coward*	153	
Millwork	*Working*	216	
Moments in the Woods	*Into The Woods*	100	
The Music Still Plays On	*A New Brain*	145	

Song Title	Show	Page	Vocal Range

Song Title	Show	Page
My Cousin in Milwaukee	Pardon My English	180
My Own Best Friend	Chicago	24
Notice Me Horton	Seussical the Musical	187
Old Friend	I'm Getting My Act Together and Taking It on the Road	94
Over the Rainbow	The Wizard of Oz	211
Something of My Own	Dessa Rose	52
Somewhere That's Green	Little Shop of Horrors	116
Take It on the Chin	Me and My Girl	133
Tell Me Why	A Man of No Importance	130
That Mister Man of Mine	Dames At Sea	37
Think of Meryl Streep	Fame: The Musical	72
West End Avenue	The Magic Show	122
What Is a Woman?	I Do, I Do	89
What a Nice Idea	Two Gentlemen of Verona	197
Wonderful, Wonderful Day	Seven Brides For Seven Brothers	193
Zip	Pal Joey	175

Introduction

Within the opening pages, you will find a synopsis of the plot, the context of the song in each show, the name of the cast member who sang the song in the original production, song type, suggested 16-bar cuts, as well as standard information such as the show creators, and the dates and theaters of the New York runs. The vocal range for each song can be found in the Table of Contents. Below are some helpful hints for the singing actor.

Choosing a Song for an Audition

When choosing a song to sing for an audition, ask yourself the following:

1. *Would I ever play the role of the character singing this song?* If not, and you want to sing the song anyway, find a way to make it your own; create your own context after being fully informed about the original context.

2. *Does this song show off my vocal range?* Use the vocal ranges in the Table of Contents to quickly identify the highest and lowest notes in each song and to determine if they are notes you can sing comfortably.

3. *Is this song appropriate for the show for which I am auditioning?* Use the dates of the first run of each show to determine its era, then compare the era of the song to the era of the show for which you are auditioning; songs from the same era are often similar in style. But, also remember that some later composers write in the style of a previous era or write in various styles. Therefore, if you listen to a recording of the show for which you are auditioning and then listen to the songs you might choose, you can determine if the styles are similar. Singing a song from another show by the same composer who wrote the show for which you are auditioning, can be an even better way to go. If the character who sings your audition song is similar to the character for which you are auditioning, that will help the people on the other side of the table better

imagine you in the role. Also, be sure that the song type complies with what is requested in the audition notice.

4. *How do I know if this song is the right type?* Audition notices often ask for a ballad, an uptempo number, a patter song, a comedy number, standard Broadway, legit musical theatre, etc. We have suggested song-type categories for each song. Though a single song may often fall into more than one category, our type categories will serve as a helpful guide.

5. *The audition notice asks for 16 bars; which 16 bars should I sing?* There are many possibilities within each song for usable 16-bar sections. We have suggested one or two possibilities for each song that make sense in terms of the music and the lyrics, and will show range. But, remember to always learn the entire song; you may be asked to go back and sing all of it after singing your 16 bars.

Have fun at your audition! The time is yours; own it.

The Bottom Line

There is no substitute for a good vocal coach. Go to him or her with your ideas based on the above suggestions, and he or she can hone in on what will be best for you.

—Barbara Irvine

Barbara Irvine lived in New York City for 15 years, working as a music director/vocal coach/pianist/music copyist/arranger/ transcriber/transposer. She has worked with nearly all the major Broadway composers of her time there, as well as with many of the Broadway stars.

Notes

Warning: the paragraphs about the shows may contain plot spoilers.

Any actor mentioned as having originally played a role is from the opening-night cast, unless otherwise indicated.

Some of the suggested 16-bar cuts are slightly longer or shorter than exactly 16 bars in order to create complete sections. Most often, these cuttings will still be accepted at auditions asking for 16 bars. You might choose to use a bar or two preceding the cut as an introduction, or simply ask the audition pianist for a "bell tone" to use as your starting pitch; the latter is more customary and time saving. Bar numbers are indicated as m. #, e. g. bar 16 is indicated as m. 16.

Chicago

The Show

Chicago is based on a 1926 play by Maurine Dallas Watkins, a Chicago Tribune reporter who had covered the trials of several murderesses in 1924. The musical is a satire of corruption in the criminal justice system, and of the public's mania for celebrity criminals. At the beginning of the story, we learn that Roxie Hart has murdered her lover, Fred Casely. She is able to convince her husband Amos that Casely was actually a burglar, and Amos claims responsibility for the murder. But the truth soon comes out, and Roxie is arrested and sent to jail. There she meets Velma Kelly, a vaudevillian who killed her own sister, and several other murderesses. Velma is soon threatened by Roxie's media appeal and by the fact that she's hired the same lawyer, the charismatic Billy Flynn. With Flynn's help and media savvy, Roxie soon eclipses Velma as Chicago's number one celebrity murderess. Once on trial, Flynn's showmanship and his coaching of Roxie lead to her acquittal. But as the verdict is announced, the press is enticed away by the revelation of new, even more sensational crime in town. Roxie finds herself a has-been, but soon teams up with Velma in a vaudevillian "sister act."

The Authors

Music by John Kander; Lyrics by Fred Ebb; Book by Fred Ebb and Bob Fosse. Based on the play *Chicago* by Maurine Dallas Watkins.

New York Runs

June 3, 1975–August 27, 1977 at the 46th Street Theatre. The roles of Roxie Hart and Velma Kelly were originated by Gwen Verdon and Chita Rivera, respectively. The first Broadway revival opened on November 14, 1996 at the Richard Rodgers Theatre, and is still running as of this publication. The opening night cast for this revival included Ann Reinking as Roxie and Bebe Neuwirth as Velma. The film version, directed by Rob Marshall, was released in 2002 and won the Academy Award for Best Picture.

The Song

"My Own Best Friend"

After Velma fails to convince Roxie to join her old Vaudevillian sister act, Roxie learns that her fame has been eclipsed by the latest husband-murdering wife to hit the headlines. Both Roxie and Velma separately realize they can count on no one but themselves, and sing "My Own Best Friend" as a "duet"—really, simultaneous soliloquies, as each is unaware of the other in the song. This leads to Roxie's plan to feign pregnancy in order to grab her place back in the headlines, which ends Act I.

Song Type

Contemporary Musical Theater Mid-Tempo Ballad (Kander and Ebb torch song/anthem)

Suggested 16-Bar Cut for Auditions

m.62 (including pick-up) to m.77.

Closer Than Ever

The Show

Like their earlier show *Starting Here, Starting Now, Closer Than Ever* is a two-act revue of Maltby and Shire songs, some of which had previously appeared in their book musicals. With humor and poignancy, each song stands alone as a story, exploring adult issues such as getting older, facing mid-life, second marriages, parent-child conflicts and grieving the lost chances of youth.

The Authors

Music by David Shire; Lyrics by Richard Maltby, Jr. Conceived by Steven Scott Smith. "Back on Base" was originally sung by Sally Mayes in this production.

New York Run

October 17, 1989–July 1, 1990 at the
Cherry Lane Theatre.

The Song

"Back on Base"

"Back on Base" is a playful jazz/blues number
that was originally performed as a duet between a
female singer and the show's actual (male) upright
bass player. It seems that the woman finds bliss in
her amorous relations with a bass-player, feeling
"back on base" in her life as a result. But when *he*
is "back on *bass*," she finds herself competing for
his affections with a musical instrument.

Song Type

Contemporary Musical Theater Uptempo with a
jazzy/bluesy feel.

Suggested 16-Bar Cut for Auditions

m. 27 through the downbeat of m. 43. This is the
first "Bridge" of the song. The accompanist can
play a low G bass "sting" on beat three of m. 43
(in lieu of what's written) to finish it out.

Dames At Sea

The Show

This musical is both an homage to and send-up
of 1930's Warner Brothers movie musicals like
42nd Street and *Dames*. In the story, theatrical
producer/manager Hennesy struggles to keep
his latest Broadway musical afloat, thanks to
difficulties brought about by the Depression and
by the show's diva star, Mona Kent. Enter young
tap-dancer Ruby, fresh off the bus from Utah
and determined to become a Broadway star. She
befriends the sassy chorus girl Joan, and falls for
Dick, a sailor and aspiring songwriter. Ruby lands
a job in the chorus, but Hennesy soon announces
that the WPA must tear down the theatre before
the show can open. Dick and his sailor buddy
Lucky convince their Captain—an old flame of
Mona's—to allow the cast to rehearse and perform
the musical on board their ship. While rehearsing
on deck, Mona becomes violently sea sick;
Ruby steps in to replace her at the last minute
and becomes a star. In the end, the Captain and
Mona, Joan and Lucky, and Ruby and Dick are all
married and live happily ever after.

The Authors

Music by Jim Wise; Book and Lyrics by
George Haimsohn and Robin Miller.

New York Runs

Off-Broadway, December 20, 1968–May 10,
1970, first at the Bouwerie Lane Theatre, then the
Theatre De Lys (now the Lucille Lortel Theatre).
Tamara Long originated the role of Mona. The
show was revived at the Lamb's Theatre in 1985,
and again at the Bouwerie Lane Theatre in 2004.

The Song

"That Mister Man of Mine"

Early in the play, diva star Mona Kent sets her
sights on the young and talented Dick, and
convinces him to give her one of his songs to
sing. Eager for his music to be brought into the
Big Time, Dick accompanies Mona as she learns
and sings "That Mister Man of Mine" in a private
performance for him.

Song Type

Standard Musical Theater Ballad (Comic) with
a Torch Song/Blues feel (1930's homage)

Suggested 16-Bar Cut for Auditions

m. 64 to the end (m. 80). Another option is
m. 17 through m. 36 if you would like to use a
lower vocal range; in this case, the accompanist
would need to play a sustained tonic chord (B-flat)
on the downbeat of m. 36, as you sustain your last
note. This version is 20 bars, which is generally
acceptable for a 16-bar audition.

Damn Yankees

The Show

Damn Yankees is the story of Joe Boyd, a middle-
aged real estate salesman and baseball fanatic.
Frustrated that his favorite team, the Washington
Senators, always loses the pennant to the Yankees,
Joe swears that he would sell his soul to the devil
if it meant victory for the Senators. In a flash,
smooth-talking Mr. Applegate appears and offers
to transform Joe into a great ballplayer for the
Senators—if Joe will indeed promise his soul.
After arranging an "out clause" with Applegate,
Joe is transformed into young Joe Hardy, a
spectacular athlete who soon leads the Senators

on a winning streak. However, Joe misses his wife, Meg, and rents a room from her as a young man whom she fails to recognize as her husband. Applegate, concerned that Joe's love for his wife will break their deal, employs sexy temptress Lola to try and seduce Joe away from Meg. The plan fails, and Lola develops a friendly affection for Joe that helps him realize his dream with the Senators *and* save his soul, much to Applegate's fury. At the end of the play, Joe returns happily to his middle-aged life with Meg.

The Authors
Music and Lyrics by Richard Adler and Jerry Ross; Book by George Abbott and Douglass Wallopp; from the novel *The Year the Yankees Lost the Pennant* by Douglass Wallopp.

New York Run
May 5, 1955–May 4, 1957 at the 46th Street Theatre; May 6–October 12, 1957 at the Adelphi Theatre. The role of Lola was originated by Gwen Verdon. The show was revived in 1994 at the Marquis Theatre (with script revisions by Jack O'Brien) and featured Bebe Neuwirth as Lola.

The Song
"A Little Brains, A Little Talent"
Applegate, realizing that he needs to distract Joe and lure him away from Meg, calls upon Lola, his number one seductress, to do the job. Lola is actually an ancient old witch who appears to be a young, sexy vamp. When Applegate pitches his latest assignment for Lola and asks if she's capable, Lola responds with "A Little Brains, A Little Talent"—a song in which she enumerates her successes as a femme fatale through the ages.

Song Type
Standard Musical Theater Comic Uptempo

Suggested 16-Bar Cut for Auditions
m. 51 through m. 66 (the accompanist should end with the vocal on beat 2 of m. 66). Another option would be m. 103 to m. 123; this is 21 bars, but as the song is an Uptempo, it shouldn't feel too long, and it would have a "bigger finish." The accompanist can sustain beat 2 of m. 123 to finish out the song without adding more measures.

Dessa Rose

The Show
Based on the novel by Sherley Anne Williams—which in turn was based on the lives of actual historical figures—*Dessa Rose* is the story of two women from very different backgrounds, living in the American South in 1847. The story is told by the women when they are elderly; they reflect on their younger years and transform into their younger selves as scenes from the past unfold. The young Dessa Rose is a 16-year-old pregnant slave girl who attacks her master after he kills the baby's father. She is sold to a slave trader and tries to escape, but is caught and sentenced to death; she is only allowed to live until her baby is born. While in prison, she is interviewed by Adam Nehemiah, a white man who is interested in slave rebellions, and who finds himself more and more interested in Dessa Rose. Meanwhile, the character of Ruth, a privileged southern belle, is introduced. She marries well and moves to a large plantation in Alabama, but is soon abandoned by her husband. After Dessa Rose is freed from prison by her companions, they all escape and seek shelter with Ruth on her isolated plantation. Ruth delivers Dessa Rose's child, and the two women forge an unlikely friendship that grows deeper as they learn to trust each other and understand both their differences and their similarities. Eventually, Ruth helps Dessa Rose and her companions escape to the slave-free West, although their plans are almost thwarted by the obsessive Nehemiah.

The Authors
Music by Stephen Flaherty; Lyrics by Lynn Ahrens; Book by Sherley Anne Williams

New York Run
March 21, 2005–May 29, 2005 at the Mitzi E. Newhouse Theatre. The role of Dessa Rose was originated by LaChanze.

The Song
"Something of My Own"
Early in the story, in the slaves' quarters, Dessa Rose reveals that she is pregnant with her man Kaine's baby. Her mother, Rose, does not want her to have the child, but Dessa Rose is passionate about keeping it--a conviction she expresses to both her mother and Kaine in "Something of My Own."

Song Type

Contemporary Musical Theater Ballad (with a Southern Folk feel). While the song is in cut time and the accompaniment has a drive to it, the lines of the vocal are often long and sustained, making it more of a Ballad than an Uptempo.

Suggested 16-Bar Cut for Auditions

m. 44 to m. 64. This is 21 bars, but shouldn't feel too long for a 16-bar audition. The accompanist can sustain a D chord (no 5th) on the downbeat of m. 64 to finish out the song without adding measures.

Destry Rides Again

The Show

Based on the classic 1939 Hollywood Western comedy starring James Stewart and Marlene Dietrich, *Destry Rides Again* centers on the corrupt town of Bottleneck and its new deputy sheriff, Thomas Jefferson Destry, Jr.—the son of a famous gunfighter, and a man who abhors violence and guns. Destry is brought in to help Wash, the town drunk who is named as the new sheriff after the old sheriff is mysteriously murdered. In the process of trying to help solve this murder, Destry is introduced to Frenchy, a saloon-hall entertainer who also happens to be the gal of Kent, a card sharp involved in the murder. Kent tries to put Destry off the scent by getting Frenchy to seduce him, but this backfires; Destry ultimately solves the murder, cleans up the town, and unites in love with the repentant Frenchy.

The Authors

Music and Lyrics by Harold Rome; Book by Leonard Gershe. Based on the story by Max Brand.

New York Run

April 23, 1959–June 18, 1960 at the Imperial Theatre. The role of Frenchy was originated by Delores Gray; the role of Destry was originated by Andy Griffith.

The Song

"Ladies"

In the first act, "Ladies" is sung by Frenchy and the girls as a saloon-hall number that manages to both admonish and seduce the bar's male clientele.

Song Type

Standard Musical Theater Comic Ballad

Suggested 16-Bar Cut for Auditions

m. 44 (including pick-up) to the end (m. 59).

Elton John and Tim Rice's "Aida"

The Show

Based on Verdi's oft-performed classic grand Opera set in ancient Egypt, John and Rice's *Aida* is a Pop/Rock version of the same story. Aida is a Nubian princess who is captured by soldiers and brought to Egypt as a slave. Radames, the soldiers' powerful commander, falls in love with her and struggles to choose between this love and his loyalty to the Pharaoh. To complicate matters, Radames is loved by and betrothed to Amneris, the Pharaoh's daughter. Ultimately inspired by Aida's courage and love for her people, Radames aids the Nubians, and he and Aida are sentenced to death by the Pharaoh. Amneris convinces her father to allow her to sentence them to be buried alive in a tomb beneath the sands of Egypt. Once there, Aida and Radames vow to find each other even if they have to search for "a hundred lifetimes". The play ends with the souls of the two lovers re-uniting as a modern-day couple in the Egyptian wing of a contemporary museum.

The Authors

Music by Elton John; Lyrics by Tim Rice; Book by Linda Woolverton, Robert Falls and David Henry Hwang. Based on the opera by Giuseppe Verdi.

New York Run

March 23, 2000–September 5, 2004 at the Palace Theatre. The role of Amneris was originated by Sherie Rene Scott; the role of Radames was originated by Adam Pascal.

The Song

"I Know the Truth"

In the second act, Radames tells Aida that he plans to call off his wedding with Amneris in order to be with her, but Aida convinces him that in spite of their love for each other, they could never have a life together. Radames vows to arrange for Aida's escape to Nubia during his wedding. Soon after the lovers leave, Amneris emerges from the shadows, having seen everything. As her attendants dress her for her wedding, she admits that she is not Radames' true love in "I Know the Truth."

Song Type

Contemporary Musical Theater Pop/Rock Ballad.

Suggested 16-Bar Cut for Auditions

m. 48 to the end (m. 65). This is 18 bars, which is generally acceptable for a 16-bar audition.

Falsettos

The Show

Falsettos is comprised of two one-act musicals that are part of William Finn's "Marvin Trilogy"—three sung-through plays focusing on Marvin, his wife Trina, his young son Jason, and his male lover, Whizzer. In Act I (originally *March of the Falsettos*), it is 1979, and Marvin is determined to maintain a "Tight-Knit Family" in spite of the fact that he wishes to live with Whizzer as well as his enraged wife and confused son. He seeks the help of his psychiatrist, Mendel, who makes matters worse by moving in on, and becoming involved with Trina. In the end, Marvin loses Trina, Mendel and Whizzer, but is hopeful that his relationship with his son is still viable. In Act II (originally *Falsettoland*), it is 1981, Jason is preparing for his bar mitzvah amidst quarrelling parents, and Whizzer—having gotten back together with Marvin—succumbs to a mysterious new disease, yet to be identified as AIDS. In the end, Jason helps reunite everyone by demanding that his bar mitzvah be held in Whizzer's hospital room.

The Authors

Music and Lyrics by William Finn; Book by William Finn and James Lapine.

New York Run

On Broadway, April 29, 1992–June 27, 1993 at the John Golden Theatre. Barbara Walsh portrayed Trina in this production. Originally produced off-Broadway as two separate shows, *March of the Falsettos* (with Alison Frasier as Trina) and *Falsettoland* (with Faith Prince as Trina).

The Song

"Holding to the Ground"

In Act II, once it is clear that Whizzer is very ill and that his prognosis is not good, Trina sings "Holding to the Ground." In spite of her upbringing and lingering anger at Marvin, she discovers that she has compassion for both Whizzer and her husband, and she fights to maintain control and a positive outlook in this devastating situation.

Song Type

Contemporary Musical Theater Dramatic Uptempo

Suggested 16-Bar Cut for Auditions

Since the song is in cut time, it should be permissable to sing m. 18 (including pick-up) through m. 49, which is 32 bars—or the equivalent of 16 bars in $\frac{4}{4}$. To finish out the song, the accompanist can play a sustained tonic (C) in lieu of the written bar 50. Sustain the note on "Life" through this, as you wouldn't be singing "I'm plain" to continue; and it's usually a good idea for the piano and voice to end together.

Fame: The Musical

The Show

Based on the popular musical film of 1980, *Fame—the Musical* follows a group of diverse and talented students attending New York's High School for the Performing Arts in the early 1980's. Characters include Carmen Diaz, a fiery Latina dancer with her eyes on Hollywood; Schlomo Metzenbaum, her shy violinist friend; Nick Piazza, a handsome, serious actor; Serena Katz, an insecure actress in love with Nick; and Tyrone Jackson, a street-wise hip-hop dancer who is illiterate. As the students experience the highs and lows of their life at "P.A.," they confront issues such as racism, literacy, sexuality, drug abuse, identity and perseverance. From audition to graduation, they grow as artists and as human beings, and ultimately look toward the future with hopeful determination.

The Authors

Music by Steve Margoshes; Lyrics by Jacques Levy; Book by Jose Fernandez. Based on the film by Alan Parker.

New York Run

Off-Broadway, November 11, 2003–June 27, 2004 at the Little Schubert Theatre. The official title for this production was *Fame on 42nd Street*. Nicole Leach originated the role of Carmen Diaz in this production; Rick Cornette played Nick Piazza, and Sara Schmidt played Serena Katz.

The Song

"Think of Meryl Streep"

After landing the role of Juliet in the school production of "Romeo and Juliet," Serena is disappointed to learn that Nick, the object of her affection, has not been cast as Romeo. She complains to a fellow student, who informs her that Nick is gay. Nick learns of this, tells Serena he is not gay, and that in fact sex is not a priority for him. Upset and confused by all of this, Serena sings "Think of Meryl Streep" in an attempt to channel her intense emotions into her acting.

Song Type

Contemporary Musical Theater Uptempo

Suggested 16-Bar Cut for Auditions

m. 45 to the end (m. 62). This equals 18 bars, which is generally acceptable for a 16-bar audition (and two of the measures are in $\frac{2}{4}$, making it the equivalent of 17 bars). You could also try using "the Bridge" (m. 28 through m. 43). This doesn't end on a "home chord," but shows off the high belting range sooner, if that's a priority.

Gentlemen Prefer Blondes

The Show

Most notable as the Broadway musical that launched the career of Carol Channing, *Gentlemen Prefer Blondes* is the Roaring Twenties story of Lorelei Lee, a gold-digging blonde party girl, and her wise-cracking friend and fellow showgirl, brunette Dorothy Shaw. The two head for Paris on an ocean liner, with Lorelei seeking wealthy eligible men, and Dorothy seeking the type of fun with men that doesn't necessarily involve their bank accounts. Complicating matters is Lorelei's engagement to a wealthy American button-making heir, the presence of the American

Olympic team, and a dazzling diamond tiara that Lorelei is loathe to live without. In 1953, *Gentlemen Prefer Blondes* was released as a film starring Marilyn Monroe and Jane Russell.

The Authors

Music by Jule Styne; Lyrics by Leo Robin; Book by Joseph Fields and Anita Loos. Adapted from the novel by Anita Loos.

New York Runs

December 8, 1949–September 15, 1951 at the Ziegfeld Theatre. Carol Channing originated the role of Lorelei Lee. The show was revived at the Lyceum Theatre in 1995, featuring KT Sullivan as Lorelei Lee.

The Song

"A Little Girl from Little Rock"

Early in the play, Lorelei introduces herself and sings of how she evolved from naïve Arkansas gal to luxury-loving New York coquette in "A Little Girl from Little Rock." Along with "Diamonds Are a Girl's Best Friend" (also from *Gentlemen Prefer Blondes*), this number is considered one of Carol Channing's "signature songs."

Song Type

Standard Musical Theater Uptempo

Suggested 16-Bar Cut for Auditions

m. 65 (including pick-ups) through m. 81; then cut m. 82 to m. 89, go right to m. 90 and finish the song as written (through m. 94). This is 22 bars in cut time, which is the equivalent of 11 bars in $\frac{4}{4}$. You could get away with keeping bars 82 to 89 (equaling 30 bars in cut time), but this would most likely feel too repetitive in a 16-bar cutting.

The Golden Apple

The Show

The Golden Apple is a sung-through musical comedy adaptation of Homer's epic poems of the Trojan War, *The Iliad* and *The Odyssey*. The authors created interlocking production numbers and used American popular song styles to tell this classic story in a folksy American setting—the state of Washington at the turn of the 20th century. Ulysses and his men are returning veterans of the Spanish-American War, Penelope is Ulysses' long-suffering, patient wife, and Helen is the impatient wife of older Sheriff Menelaus. The Olympian goddesses are cast as high-powered townswomen, whose Judgment of Paris takes the form of a pie-baking contest; Paris is the handsome traveling salesman they choose as their impartial judge. By the end of Act I (*The Iliad*), Paris has abducted Helen in his hot air balloon, and the older townsmen (led by Menelaus) pressure the younger men (led by Ulysses) to go to war in the big city to avenge Helen's abduction. Act II (*The Odyssey*) begins with an unexpectedly quick reunion of Helen and Menelaus; Ulysses and his men decide to stay on in the big city, but their "spree" turns into a 10-year nightmare of death and destruction, as all the men except Ulysses succumb to the wicked city's temptations. A war-weary Ulysses returns to Penelope and vows to her that he is home to stay. She forgives him and they face their future together.

The Authors

Music by Jerome Moross; lyrics by John Latouche.

New York Runs

Off-Broadway: Opened March 11, 1954 at the Phoenix Theatre. Transferred to Broadway, playing at the Alvin Theatre, April 20th–August 7, 1954. Both productions featured Priscilla Gillette as Penelope, Stephen Douglass as Ulysses, and Kaye Ballard as Helen.

The Song

"Lazy Afternoon"

Townswoman Lovey Mars--patterned after the Greek goddess of Love Aphrodite--promises traveling salesman Paris a future of adoring, beautiful women at his beck and call. Excited by this prospect, he awards her first prize in the ladies' pie-baking contest. To make good on her promise, Lovey quickly introduces Paris to Helen, a married woman who nonetheless has reputation of "easy virtue" among the townsmen. Helen sings "Lazy Afternoon" in order to seduce Paris. She succeeds, and Paris soon steals her away in his hot air balloon.

Song type

Standard Musical Theater Ballad, with a bluesy feel.

Suggested 16-Bar Cut for Auditions

m. 48 (including pick-up) to m. 66. This equals 19 bars; up to 20 bars is generally acceptable for a 16-bar audition.

I Do! I Do!

The Show

This intimate two-character musical traces the 50-year history of a married couple, Agnes and Michael. They begin as nervous young newlyweds and end as contented septuagenarians; in between, they raise a family, survive an affair and mid-life crises, argue, make up and learn to grow old together. Each scene takes place in their bedroom, with a large fourposter bed as its centerpiece.

The Authors

Music by Harvey Schmidt; Book and Lyrics by Tom Jones. Based on *The Fourposter* by Jan De Hartog.

New York Run

December 5, 1966–June 15, 1968 at the 46th Street Theatre. The role of Agnes was originated by Mary Martin; the role of Michael was originated by Robert Preston.

The Song

"What Is a Woman?"

In the second act, Agnes and Michael's daughter gets married, and each experiences a different reaction to the event: before the wedding, Michael is angry that his daughter "is marrying an idiot;" after the wedding, Agnes feels depressed and lonely as she faces growing older, in "What Is a Woman?"

Song Type

Standard Musical Theater Ballad.

Suggested 16-Bar Cut for Auditions

m. 49 (including pick-ups) to the end (m. 65). This is 17 bars, plus a bass "sting." Another option is m. 31 through m. 46, especially if singing in a lower key is desired. This is 16 bars total, although the accompanist would need to play the tonic chord of C major to finish out the song after m. 46.

I'm Getting My Act Together And Taking It On The Road

The Show

It is performer Heather Jones' 39th birthday, and she is rehearsing her new cabaret act with her band, the Liberated Men. Joe, her old friend and manager, arrives to listen to Heather's new material and becomes more and more uncomfortable with what he sees and hears. The "old Heather" performed songs that portrayed woman in more traditional and subservient roles; Heather's new songs encourage women to be independent and powerful, and Joe is afraid that her audience will be put off by them. As the rehearsal proceeds and Heather and Joe's arguments become more heated, it is revealed that Heather is recently divorced, and that Joe's wife has attempted suicide. Joe persists in trying to convince Heather to go back to performing her old act, and Heather ultimately realizes that her old friend will never accept her as a "new woman." She tells Joe to leave, and begins to face her new act—and life—without him.

The Authors

Music by Nancy Ford; Book and Lyrics by Gretchen Cryer.

New York Run

Off-Broadway, May 16, 1978–March 15, 1981 at the Joseph Papp Public Theatre/Anspacher Theatre. The role of Heather was originated by Gretchen Cryer.

The Song

"Old Friend"

At one point, Joe becomes so angry and offended by Heather's new act that he storms out of the room. He returns to explain his point of view, and they seem to find some common ground. Heather sings "Old Friend," a new song she has written about her friendship with Joe, and he finds himself deeply touched by it.

Song Type
Contemporary Musical Theater Folk/Pop Ballad

Suggested 16-Bar Cut for Auditions
m. 55 (including pick-ups) to the end (m. 72). This is 18 bars, which is generally acceptable for a 16-bar audition.

Into The Woods

The Show

In *Into the Woods*, several classic fairy tale characters' lives intersect with an original story: that of The Baker and His Wife. Cinderella, Little Red Riding Hood, Jack (of beanstalk fame) and Rapunzel all become important to the couple as the two strive to undo a witch's curse that prevents them from having a child. The witch herself is cursed with old age and ugliness, and promises the couple she will reverse their situation if they can gather the ingredients for a potion that would restore her youth and beauty. As it happens, each of the other fairy tale characters possesses one of the potion's ingredients, but as they are all in the thick of their own stories, acquiring said ingredients proves almost impossible for the Baker and his Wife. By the end of Act I, however, the potion is successfully created, the curses are reversed, and all live happily "Ever After"…or do they? Act II of *Into the Woods* explores what happens *after* "Happily Ever After;" the wife of Jack's slain Giant comes back to seek revenge, and all must unite in order to save themselves from annihilation. In the process, they learn some hard truths about their previous actions, and must face the fact that their lives are inescapably interconnected.

The Authors

Music and Lyrics by Stephen Sondheim; Book by James Lapine.

New York Runs

November 5, 1987–September 3, 1989. The role of the Witch was originated by Bernadette Peters; the role of the Baker's Wife was originated by Joanna Gleason. The show was revived in 2002 at the Broadhurst Theatre, with Vanessa Williams as the Witch and Kerry O'Malley as the Baker's Wife.

The Songs

"Moments in the Woods"

In Act II, Rapunzel is accidentally killed by the Giant's Wife, who has been seeking vengeance for her husband's death. Rapunzel's mother—the now-beautiful Witch—decides that Jack must be offered up to the Giantess as a sacrifice. The Baker and his Wife, however, are determined to protect Jack, and go off in opposite directions to search for him. Along the way, the Baker's Wife encounters Cinderella's Prince, and is ultimately seduced by him, then left by herself. "Moments in the Woods" is a sung soliloquy in which she assesses what just happened, and determines that—in spite of the excitement and allure of the previous moment— she must return to her commitment as a wife and mother.

Song Type

Contemporary Musical Theater Midtempo/Ballad

Suggested 16-Bar Cut for Auditions

m. 74 (including pick-ups) to the end (m. 93). This is 20 bars, which is generally acceptable for a 16-bar audition.

"Last Midnight"

In Act II, the Baker learns that his wife has been killed by the Giantess, and soon he, Little Red Riding Hood, Jack and Cinderella are all blaming each other for the Giant woman's destructive presence in their lives. The Witch responds to them with the tirade "Last Midnight."

Song Type

Contemporary Musical Theater Dramatic Uptempo

Suggested 16-Bar Cut for Auditions

m. 74 (including pick-ups) to the end (m. 93). This equals 20 bars, which is generally acceptable for a 16-bar audition.)

Little Shop Of Horrors

The Show

Based on the campy cult horror film by Roger Corman, *Little Shop of Horrors* is the Faustian tale of Seymour Krelborn, a lowly assistant in Mushnik's floral shop on Skid Row in the early 1960's. Browbeaten by his boss and too shy to express his affections for lovely co-worker Audrey, things seem hopeless for Seymour--until he acquires a mysterious fly-trap-like plant that he discovers can only survive by consuming human blood. The plant, which Seymour names Audrey II after his secret love, grows exponentially from drops of blood from Seymour's pricked fingers. This brings attention and eventually fame and prosperity to Seymour and to Mushnik's shop; but soon Audrey II grows larger and demands that Seymour feed him human flesh, promising him his heart's desires if he can comply. After Seymour feeds Audrey's abusive dentist boyfriend to the insatiable plant, things start to get out of control. Seymour wins more fame, and the love of Audrey, but Audrey II ultimately destroys all that he has strived for.

The Authors

Music by Alan Mencken; Book and Lyrics by Howard Ashman.

New York Run

Off-Broadway: July 27, 1982–November 1, 1987 at the Orpheum Theatre. Audrey was originally portrayed by Ellen Greene, who reprised the role in the 1986 film version directed by Frank Oz.

The Song

"Somewhere That's Green"

In the first act, still suffering from her sadistic boyfriend's recent abuses, Audrey dreams of her ideal suburban life—far from Skid Row—in "Somewhere That's Green."

Song Type

Contemporary Musical Theater Comic Ballad.

Suggested 16-Bar Cut for Auditions

m. 59 (including pick-up) through m. 76. To avoid adding extra measures, use m. 78–m. 79 as the "rideout" under the vocal sung in m. 76. This would be 19 bars altogether (generally acceptable for a 16-bar audition).

The Magic Show

The Show

The Magic Show was a vehicle for Doug Henning, a popular magician of the 1970's and early 1980's. The story is set in a run-down nightclub that features an aging magician (Feldman the Magnificent) who is drunk all the time; the nightclub's manager decides to bring in a younger, less conventional magician named Doug, and a rivalry with Feldman ensues. As Doug begins to perform his act at the club, it becomes clear that his girl assistant Cal is love with him, in vain. Meanwhile, the nightclub also features a singing rock duo, Donna and Dina. Through a connection, the duo is able to bring in a high-powered agent named Goldfarb to view the club's acts. Ever ambitious, Doug decides he needs to conjure up a more beautiful assistant, which angers Cal. Enter the gorgeous new assistant, Charmin, who convinces everyone that Goldfarb will love Doug's act because of her looks. Donna, Dina and Feldman scheme to expose Doug's magic secrets during his act, but they fail. In the end, Doug realizes he really loves Cal, and they reunite.

The Authors

Music and Lyrics by Stephen Schwartz; Book by Bob Randall

New York Run

May 28, 1974–December 31, 1978 at the Cort Theatre. The role of Cal was originated by Dale Soules.

The Song

"West End Avenue"

After Doug declares that he needs a beautiful assistant, an angry Cal decides to leave and return to her former home, on "West End Avenue."

Song Type

Contemporary Musical Theater Uptempo (Pop)

Suggested 16-Bar Cut for Auditions

m. 91 (including pick-up) to the end (m. 120). This is 28 bars, but the song goes at such a fast clip that it shouldn't feel too long for a 16-bar audition. NOTE: The many meter changes (and irregular meters) that Mr. Schwartz has written may be daunting to an accompanist who is not familiar with the music.

A Man Of No Importance

The Show

Based on the 1994 movie starring Albert Finney, *A Man of No Importance* is set in Dublin, Ireland in the 1960's. Alfie Byrne, a bus driver and avid fan of poetry and literature—especially the works of Oscar Wilde—is staging Wilde's controversial play *Salome* at his church, over the objections of the church authorities. His unmarried sister Lily is pressuring Alfie to wed so that she can stop having to take care of him and get married herself; however, Alfie is secretly not attracted to women romantically, and instead feels drawn to his handsome young co-worker Robbie. As Alfie continues to fight for the life of *Salome*, he gains the courage to become who he really is inside, and ultimately faces the future with those who love him unconditionally.

The Authors

Music by Stephen Flaherty; Lyrics by Lynn Ahrens; Book by Terrance McNally.

New York Run

October 10–December 29, 2002 at the Mitzi E. Newhouse Theatre. The role of Lily Byrne was originated by Faith Prince; the role of Alfie Byrne was originated by Roger Rees.

The Song

"Tell Me Why"

Alfie, finally deciding to act on his attraction to men, is lured from a pub by a young man, only to be beaten by him and his companions. The word spreads through the community that Alfie is gay. The next morning at breakfast, Alfie is badly bruised, and Lily expresses her hurt and confusion about his secrecy in "Tell Me Why"—in the end admonishing him for not realizing that she would love him no matter what.

Song Type

Contemporary Musical Theater Ballad with an Irish folk song feel.

Suggested 16-Bar Cut for Auditions

m. 28 (including pick-ups) to the end (m. 37). This equals 10 bars. Another option is m. 18 (including pick-ups) to the end. This equals 20 bars, which is generally acceptable for a 16-bar audition.

Me And My Girl

The Show

The Broadway version of *Me and My Girl* was actually a revival of a highly successful English musical that ran in London from 1937 through the early days of World War II. As a result, the show (and its songs) has become a part of the "English national psyche." The story revolves around Bill Snibson, a low cockney bloke from Lambeth, a poor section of London. He learns that he has been named in a will as the heir to the Earl of Hareford. When the Earl's aristocratic family brings Bill to Hareford Hall to examine him, they are all put off by his lower class status; however, the formidable Duchess of Dene is determined to turn him into a gentleman, and to separate him from his cockney sweetheart Sally. In addition, the ambitious Lady Jacqueline Carstone, knowing that

Bill will soon be a Lord worth millions, moves in on him—in spite of her engagement to another man of her class. Thus begins a comic tug-of-war, as various family members try to impose their agendas upon the new heir. The Duchess eventually convinces Sally to leave Bill in order for him to become a true gentleman. But soon afterward, Uncle John helps to civilize and groom Sally as well, and she returns to Hareford Hall as a lady, worthy of the new and improved gentleman Bill. The once lowly cockney is now able to keep both his Earlship and his girl.

The Authors

Music by Noel Gay; Book and Lyrics by L. Arthur Rose and Douglas Furber. Book revised by Stephen Fry; contributions to the revisions by Mike Ockrent.

New York Run

August 10, 1986–December 31, 1989 at the Marquis Theatre. The role of Sally Smith was originated by Maryann Plunkett in this production.

The Song

"Take It on the Chin"

In the second act, Sally realizes that she must let go of Bill so that he can become a gentleman. In "Take It on the Chin," she sings of her determination to stay cheerful, in spite of her heartbreak. Her audience is the elderly Sir Jasper, who seems supportive of Sally in spite of his inability to hear what she's saying.

Song Type

Standard Musical Theater Uptempo, in the tradition of English Music Hall.

Suggested 16-Bar Cut for Auditions

m. 81 to m. 92, then cut to m. 97 and finish out the song as written (through m. 102). This equals 18 bars, which is generally acceptable for a 16-bar audition. Another option is m. 89 to the end (m. 102), which equals 14 bars all together.

Merrily We Roll Along

The Show

Based on the 1934 non-musical play by Kauffman and Hart, *Merrily We Roll Along* traces the history of Franklin Shepard—a wealthy Broadway composer and film producer—and his two close friends, Charley (his writing partner) and Mary (also a writer, whose love for Franklin is unrequited). The action of the play begins in the present and moves backward in time, revealing the choices that lead to Shepard's fame and financial success, but that ultimately destroy his close relationships. As the play proceeds and the characters grow younger (from cynical middle age to idealistic high school teenagers), the highlights of their theatrical careers are shown in rehearsals, performances and backstage glimpses of their work together. By the end of the play, it is clear that artistic compromise and a blind love of power and money can take a destructive toll on an artist and those close to him.

The Authors

Music and Lyrics by Stephen Sondheim; Book by George Furth. From the play by George S. Kauffman and Moss Hart.

New York Run

November 16–28, 1981 at the Alvin Theatre. The role of Mary Flynn was originated by Ann Morrison. There have been numerous American regional and British revivals (most incorporating changes to the original script and score), but there have been no major Broadway revivals.

The Song

"Like It Was"

Sung early in the play (but late in the history of the characters) "Like It Was" is Mary's attempt to rekindle the warmth of the "old days" when she, Charley and Franklin were young and idealistic. Alone with Charley in a restaurant, she tries to get him to see the value of what they all once had together, and hopes that he and Franklin can find reconciliation as friends. However, Charley is now completely estranged from Franklin, and Mary is alcoholic and beginning to succumb to her own bitter resignation about life.

Song Type
Contemporary Musical Theater Dramatic Ballad

Suggested 16-Bar Cut for Auditions
m. 21 (with pick-ups) to m. 35; the accompanist can sustain the downbeat of m. 35 to finish out the song. Another option is m. 43-63; this is 21 bars, which might be pushing it for a 16-bar audition. Again, the accompanist would need to sustain the downbeat of m. 63 to finish—the rideout as written would add too many measures.

A New Brain

The Show

A New Brain is William Finn's semi-autobiographical account of a songwriter who is suddenly stricken with a serious (and possibly terminal) brain condition. At the beginning of the play, Gordon Schwinn is struggling to write a song for his boss Mr. Bungee, the tyrannical frog-host of a children's television program. At lunch with his friend Rhoda, Gordon complains about not being able to do the writing he really wants to do; after Mr. Bungee appears to him as a hallucination, Gordon collapses face-first into his pasta. He is rushed to the hospital, where he is diagnosed with a rare brain condition that requires surgery. With his loved ones around him (Rhoda, his mother, and his partner, Roger), Gordon faces his mortality—and the terrifying prospect that he has "so many songs" within him that may never be written. What follows is a nightmarish and often comic odyssey in which Gordon manages to create songs in spite of his condition: in his hospital bed, while in an MRI chamber, and even while in a coma. The songs weave together bits of his past, his present, and his imagined future, all featuring a host of characters both intimate and remote to him. His imagination, creativity and sense of humor prevail and indeed seem to pull him through; in the end he survives his operation and recovers, with a renewed sense of freedom and a new perspective on his life and relationships.

The Authors
Music and Lyrics by William Finn; Book by James Lapine. The vocal arrangements were created by Jason Robert Brown.

New York Run
June 18–August 23, 1998 at the Mitzi E. Newhouse Theatre. The role of Mimi Shwinn was originated by Penny Fuller.

The Song
"The Music Still Plays On"
While in a coma, Gordon imagines he has died, and that his mother (Mimi) has survived him. In the torch song-like lament "The Music Still Plays On," Mimi expresses deep regret for her failed marriage and for the untimely death of the son she felt so close to. As originally staged, Gordon accompanies her on the piano as she sings.

Song Type
Contemporary Musical Theater Ballad

Suggested 16-Bar Cut for Auditions
m. 82 to the end (m. 98).

Oh, Coward!

The Show
Oh, Coward! is a revue of songs and texts by Noel Coward (1899 -1973), the celebrated English actor, playwright and popular song composer. The show is written to be performed by two men and one woman, and covers a wide range of material from plays and musicals that Coward penned from the 1920's through the 1960's. "Mad About the Boy" was originally an ensemble number from Coward's 1932 revue, *Words and Music*, with various female characters singing its different verses and refrains. It has since become a standard for vocalists, with notable recordings by Dinah Shore, Dinah Washington and Cleo Laine.

The Authors
Music, Lyrics and Text by Noel Coward; Conceived by Roderick Cook.

New York Run
Off-Broadway, October 4, 1972–June 17, 1973 at the New Theatre. "Mad About the Boy" was sung by Barbara Cason in this production.

The Song
"Mad About the Boy"
Like all good standards and revue songs, "Mad About the Boy" can stand on its own as a complete

"short story" outside the context of a larger plot. A woman has fallen for a male film star (some say Coward used a young James Cagney as his inspiration for "the Boy"), and she struggles to deal with what is becoming an all-consuming obsession for her. The song as printed here can be looked at in at least two ways: as the expressions of two separate characters (the first and second verse/refrains were originally written for a Society Woman and a Streetwalker, respectively); the two verse/refrains can also be seen from the point of view of one woman who has fallen from an elevated status to a lower one, because of her obsession.

Song Type
Standard Musical Theater Ballad/Standard Ballad in the tradition of Tin Pan Alley.

Suggested 16-Bar Cut for Auditions
m. 92 to the end (m. 109). This is 18 bars, which is generally acceptable for a 16-bar audition. Another option is m. 39 through m. 54, which is exactly 16 bars, but with a different lyric. Go with the lyric you prefer—both cuttings are the same melodically; the first option has a longer rideout.

Oliver!

The Show
Based on Charles Dickens' novel *Oliver Twist*, *Oliver!* is the story of a poor young orphan's odyssey in Victorian London, as he progresses from abused workhouse urchin to undertaker's assistant to member of a gang of pickpockets led by the colorful and clever Fagin. Fagin's den is overseen by the violent and cruel Bill Sikes, who is involved with Nancy, a girl of the streets. After Oliver is apprehended by the police on his first outing as a pickpocket, he is taken in by a wealthy benefactor, Mr. Brownlow. Nancy is dispatched by Fagin and Sikes to retrieve the boy, but she soon learns that Oliver is from a wealthy family, and plans to return him to Brownlow at night on London Bridge. There, Bill Sikes murders her and takes Oliver hostage, but he is chased by a mob and shot dead by the police. Oliver is returned to Mr. Brownlow, who has come to learn that the boy is actually the grandson of a dear friend of his. After its Broadway run, *Oliver!* was made into a popular film directed by Carol Reed, and won the 1968 Academy Award for Best Picture.

The Authors
Music, Lyrics and Book by Lionel Bart, adapted freely from the novel *Oliver Twist* by Charles Dickens.

New York Runs
January 6, 1963–September 12, 1964 at the Imperial Theatre; September 14, 1964–November 14, 1964 at the Shubert Theatre. The role of Nancy was originated by Georgia Brown; the role of Bet was originated by Alice Playten. This production returned to the Martin Beck Theatre in 1965, featuring Maura K. Wedge as Nancy and Donnie Smiley as Bet; the show was revived in 1984 at the Mark Hellinger Theatre with Patti Lupone as Nancy and Sarah E. Litzsinger as Bet.

The Song
"It's a Fine Life"
In the first act, after Oliver is welcomed as a new member of Fagin's gang, Nancy and her young friend Bet enter the den and proudly sing of their philosophy in "It's a Fine Life." In spite of its danger and roughness (including the violent abuse Nancy suffers from boyfriend Bill Sikes), they truly love the life they lead. It is soon after this that Nancy develops protective and motherly feelings for Oliver. Note: This song was originally a duet, with the boys joining in to echo the title refrain.

Song Type
Standard Musical Theater Uptempo

Suggested 16-Bar Cut for Auditions
m. 101 (including pick-ups) to the end (m. 119). This is 19 bars, which is generally acceptable for a 16-bar audition.

Paint Your Wagon

The Show
Set in the California wilderness in 1853, *Paint Your Wagon* focuses on widowed miner Ben Rumson, his 16-year old daughter Jennifer, and a handsome Mexican miner named Julio Valveras. In Act I, Ben accidentally discovers gold and claims the land for himself; within two months the new town of Rumson is bustling with 400 men seeking gold. Amid tensions between the female-deprived miners and Ben, Julio (forced to live and work outside of town because he is

Mexican) and Jennifer (the only female in town) fall in love. Unhappy with the alliance and facing pressure from the townsmen, Ben decides to send his daughter back East. Jennifer in turn is disgusted when her father buys himself a new wife, and she runs away after vowing to return to Julio in a year's time. Once she is gone, Julio realizes that his claim is drying up and that he must move on to seek gold elsewhere. In Act II, it is a year later; Jennifer returns and is dismayed by Julio's absence. Ben's new wife leaves him for another man, and a new gold strike 40 miles south of Rumson drains the town of all its inhabitants except for Ben and Jennifer. Eventually, a poor and broken Julio returns, is welcomed by Ben, and is reunited with Jennifer.

The Authors

Music by Frederick Loewe; Book and Lyrics by Alan Jay Lerner.

New York Run

November 12, 1951–July 19, 1952 at the Shubert Theatre. The role of Jennifer Rumson was originated by Olga San Juan; the role of Julio Valveras was originated by Tony Bavaar.

The Song

"How Can I Wait?"

In Act I, Jennifer volunteers to do Julio's laundry. This leads to frequent meetings between the couple outside of town, and within two months they are in love. At home, with only Julio's laundry at hand, Jennifer is anxious for their next meeting and dancing ecstatically with his clothes as she sings "How Can I Wait?" Ben observes this and decides to send Jennifer back East on the next stagecoach.

Song Type

Standard Musical Theater Uptempo

Suggested 16-Bar Cut for Auditions

m. 79 (including pick-up, "Oh," on last quarter note) through to the end (m. 105). This is 27 bars (plus a bass "sting") in cut time, or the equivalent of 13 ½ measures in ¢.

Pal Joey

The Show

Set in the seedy world of Chicago nightclubs in the 1940's, *Pal Joey* is the story of a young opportunistic cad who charms both an innocent chorus girl (Linda English) and an older, wealthy society woman (Vera Simpson). Vera is married, but is so taken with Joey that she sets him up with his own nightclub, Chez Joey. Joey rejects Linda in favor of Vera and her money, and it seems that he is unstoppable—that is, until someone tries to blackmail Vera by threatening to divulge her relationship with Joey to her husband. Linda helps to thwart this plot, but Vera decides to let go of Joey and the club anyway, and he is left alone.

The Authors

Music by Richard Rodgers; Lyrics by Lorenz Hart; Book by John O'Hara.

New York Run

December 25, 1940–November 29, 1941, at the Ethel Barrymore, Shubert and St. James Theatres. The role of Melba Snyder was originated by Jean Casto. The show has been revived on Broadway three times, including a successful 1952 production featuring Elaine Stritch as Melba.

The Song

"Zip"

In the second act, ambitious reporter Melba Snyder interviews Joey about his new club, and endeavors to embellish his back story in order to make her column more exciting. She sings "Zip," her account of what it was like to interview legendary stripper Gypsy Rose Lee.

Song Type

Standard Musical Theater Comic Ballad/Mid-Tempo.

Suggested 16-Bar Cut for Auditions

m. 42 to the end (second ending, m. 58-m. 59). Choose the lyrics you prefer, but use the second ending, regardless.

Pardon My English

The Show

Set in Dresden, Germany, *Pardon My English* is a musical screwball comedy that revolves around an English secret agent named Michael Bramleigh. Thanks to several unfortunate blows to his head, Bramleigh lives out an alternate personality as Golo Schmidt, the shady gangster-owner of Klub 21, a speakeasy that only serves soft drinks (which have been outlawed by the German government in order to promote the sale of alcohol). When living as Golo, Bramleigh romances Gita, Klub 21's sexy Polish chanteuse; when he is "himself," Bramleigh is enamored of the police commissioner's daughter Ilse, to whom he proposes marriage. Several episodes of mistaken identity, kidnapping—and further blows to Bramleigh's head—ensue, until all is righted and Ilse gets her man.

The Authors

Music by George Gershwin; Lyrics by Ira Gershwin; Book by Herbert Fields.

New York Run

January 20, 1933–February 25, 1933 at the Majestic Theatre. The role of Gita was originated by Lyda Roberti.

The Song

"My Cousin in Milwaukee"

"My Cousin in Milwaukee" is a cabaret-like song that Gita performs for the patrons of Klub 21.

Song Type

Standard Musical Theater/Tin Pan Alley Standard Uptempo with a jazz/blues feel.

Suggested 16-Bar Cut for Auditions

While the meter as written is "cut time," the song really doesn't work as a brisk song "in 2." It plays best as a strut-like number "in 4." Because of this, you can't get away with singing more than 20 bars for a 16-bar audition, as you could in a quick cut time or $\frac{2}{4}$. A good option is m. 69 to the end (m. 86), which equals 18 bars.

Seussical The Musical

The Show

Seussical the Musical is based on several beloved children's books by Dr. Seuss, primarily *Horton Hears a Who!* The Cat in the Hat serves as the play's narrator, and occasionally manipulates the action to stir things up. The main story revolves around Horton the Elephant; he is determined to save the people of Whoville, a town that exists on a tiny speck of dust perched upon a piece of clover. Only Horton can hear the cries of the Whos, and his friends and neighbors ridicule him for speaking to and trying to protect a seemingly insignificant dust speck. One of his neighbors—the bird Gertrude McFuzz—believes in Horton's cause, and wants to help him. Unfortunately, Horton fails to notice her, which she attributes to her meager one-feather tail. As the play proceeds, other Dr. Seuss characters and stories are woven into the action, and in the end, Whoville and its inhabitants are saved, Gertrude is noticed, and Horton hatches an Elephant Bird!

The Authors

Music by Stephen Flaherty; Lyrics by Lynn Ahrens; Book by Lynn Ahrens and Stephen Flaherty; Conceived by Ahrens, Flaherty and Eric Idle. Based on the works of Dr. Seuss.

New York Run

November 30, 2000–May 20, 2001 at the Richard Rodgers Theatre. The role of Gertrude McFuzz was originated by Janine LaManna; the role of Horton was originated by Kevin Chamberlin.

The Song

"Notice Me, Horton"

Gertrude McFuzz, believing that Horton doesn't notice her because of her uninteresting one-feather tail, takes the advice of another bird, Mayzie, and soon visits the doctor for pills that will make her tail grow. Grow it does, eventually becoming so heavy that she is no longer able to fly. Nonetheless, she pursues Horton in his struggle to save the Whos, and sings "Notice Me, Horton" in an attempt to express her love. But Horton is so consumed by his search to locate the Whos (now lost in a large field of clover) that he still fails to notice her. Ultimately, it is her valiant actions, rather than her looks, which get the elephant's attention.

Song Type
Contemporary Musical Theater Ballad (Pop)

Suggested 16-Bar Cut for Auditions
m. 55 (including pick-ups) to the end (m. 74). This is 18 bars (generally acceptable for a 16-bar audition) plus a "bass sting."

Seven Brides For Seven Brothers

The Show

Based on the classic MGM musical film of 1954, *Seven Brides for Seven Brothers* takes place in the rough-and-tumble wilderness of 1850's Oregon. Adam Pontipee is pressured by his six brothers to find a wife; since their mother died, there's been no woman to take care of the household duties on their farm. Adam travels to a small lumber town and soon meets Milly, a young waitress, in the town restaurant. A lumberjack tries to get fresh with Milly, and Adam takes him out and roughs him up. He returns and eventually proposes to Milly; she accepts, little knowing what is expected of her. Once married, Adam and Milly travel back to the Pontipee farm, where she realizes that she must oversee a wildly messy household occupied by six rowdy brothers. She considers leaving Adam, but decides to stay and try to civilize her brothers-in-law and marry them off. She prepares them as well as she can, but their presence at a town social turns into a brawl, and—each brother now smitten with a girl in town—the boys decide to return to kidnap them all and make them their brides. An avalanche forces the girls to stay on the farm for the winter, but Milly lays down the law: the house is for the girls, and the brothers must live in the barn. Eventually, the spring thaw leads to a more civilized courting, reconciliation between the brothers and the townsmen, and six brides wedding six brothers.

The Authors

Music by Gene DePaul; Lyrics by Johnny Mercer; Book by Lawrence Kasha and David Landay; New Songs and Additional Lyrics by Al Kasha and Joel Hirschhorn. Based on the MGM film, which was in turn based on *The Sobbin' Women* by Stephen Vincent Benet.

New York Run

July 8 -11, 1982 at the Alvin Theatre. The role of Milly was originated by Debby Boone; the role of Adam was originated by David-James Carroll.

The Song

"Wonderful, Wonderful Day"

Milly agrees to marry Adam soon after they've met; her girlfriends question this, and she herself can't seem to believe it. She expresses her joy— and naïve expectations about married life with Adam—in "Wonderful, Wonderful Day."

Song Type
Standard Musical Theater Uptempo (Waltz)

Suggested 16-Bar Cut for Auditions
m. 65 to the end (m. 90). This is 25 bars (plus a bass sting), but as the song is in a brisk $\frac{3}{4}$ waltz time, it should be acceptable for a 16-bar audition.

Two Gentlemen Of Verona

The Show

A rock musical based on Shakespeare's comedy of youthful love and betrayal, *Two Gentlemen of Verona* focuses on Valentine and Proteus, best friends who leave their hometown of rural Verona for the big city of Milan. There, Valentine falls in love with the Duke's daughter Sylvia, who has been promised to the wealthy but doltish Thurio. Valentine schemes to steal Sylvia away (with her consent), but his efforts are thwarted by his old friend Proteus, who has fallen for her as well—and who has abandoned his pregnant sweetheart Julia back in Verona. Proteus plans to betray Valentine by telling the Duke of his plot to kidnap his daughter. Meanwhile, the spurned Julia and her maidservant travel to Milan dressed as men in order to find Proteus and confront him. Because the musical was originally written for the New York Shakespeare Festival's Central Park performances, and toured New York City neighborhoods in 1971, the score was written to reflect the wide variety of ethnic and popular music of that time and place. Thus, there are elements of Latino, Caribbean, and African-American music in the score, as well as rock, pop, doo-wop and R & B.

The Authors

Music by Galt MacDermot; Lyrics by John Guare; Book adapted by John Guare and Mel Shapiro, from the play by William Shakespeare.

New York Run

December 1, 1971–May 20, 1973 at the St. James Theatre. The role of Julia was originated by Diana Davila; the role of Valentine was originated by Clifton Davis. The show was revived in 2005 at the Delacorte Theatre in Central Park, with Rosario Dawson as Julia and Norm Lewis as Valentine.

The Song

"What a Nice Idea"

Julia, having arrived in Milan to find that Proteus has rejected her completely and is now in love with Sylvia, sings "What a Nice Idea." Note: Julia is written as a Latina-American character; she uses both Spanish and English in her speech and lyrics.

Song Type

Contemporary Musical Theater Mid-Tempo/Ballad (Pop/Rock)

Suggested 16-Bar Cut for Auditions

m. 49 (including pick-ups) to the downbeat of m. 60. This equals 11 bars (plus an accompaniment "button"). Another option is m. 60 to the end (m. 80), especially if you're interested in using the Spanish language portion of the song. This is 21 bars, but shouldn't feel too long for a 16-bar audition.

Two On The Aisle

The Show

Two on the Aisle is a musical revue that marked the first teaming of writers Betty Comden and Adolph Green with composer Jule Styne; this team would later write such Broadway hits as *Bells Are Ringing* and *Do Re Mi*. Developed to showcase the talents of former Vaudevillian (and Cowardly Lion) Bert Lahr, *Two on the Aisle* is a series of comedy routines and musical numbers that featured both Lahr and '50's Broadway star Delores Gray.

The Authors

Music by Jule Styne; Lyrics and Sketches by Betty Comden and Adolph Green.

New York Run

July 19, 1951–March 15, 1952 at the Mark Hellinger Theatre. "If You Hadn't, But You Did" was originally sung by Delores Gray.

The Song

"If You Hadn't, But You Did"

As with most well-written revue material, "If You Hadn't, But You Did" is a song that can stand alone as a self-contained story, without the benefit of a context within a larger plot. The number begins as a woman's impassioned torch-song farewell to an unfaithful lover; at the end of this introductory verse, she pulls out a gun and shoots him. The refrain that follows is a brisk patter-song litany of all of her lover's crimes and infidelities, which ultimately justifies her own crime of passion against him. NOTE: It is customary for the patter-song refrain to be "spoke-sung;" literal adherence to the written pitches and rhythms will prove to be awkward and not as effective. Experiment—what needs to be sung, and what would better be emphasized with speaking?

Song Type

Standard Musical Theater Comic Uptempo/Patter Song. Note: the introductory verse is in the style of a Blues/Torch Song Ballad.

Suggested 16-Bar Cut for Auditions

m. 100 to the end (m. 130). This is 31 bars in cut time, which is the equivalent of 15½ bars in 4/4.

The Wizard Of Oz

The Show

Based on the classic MGM movie musical (which was in turn based on the children's book by L. Frank Baum), *The Wizard of Oz* is the story of Dorothy Gale, a young girl living on a Kansas farm with her Aunt Em and Uncle Henry. Facing threats from the evil Miss Gulch, who tries to have her dog Toto destroyed, Dorothy decides to run away. En route, she meets a traveling entertainer named Professor Marvel, who convinces her to go back home. But by the time she gets back, a cyclone has reached the farm, and Dorothy and Toto are swept up in it, inside the farmhouse.

The cyclone drops them in the wonderful world of Oz, where Dorothy discovers that her house accidentally landed on and killed a witch—the sister of the Wicked Witch of the West, who now wants revenge (and her sister's magical ruby slippers, which magically found their way on to Dorothy's feet soon after she landed in Oz). Hoping to find a way back home to Kansas, Dorothy sets out for the Emerald City to get help from the Wonderful Wizard of Oz. Along the way, she meets a Scarecrow with no brain, a Tin Man with no heart, and a Cowardly Lion without courage. Together, they find the Wizard and ultimately conquer the Wicked Witch of the West, who has tried to thwart them at every turn. All acquire their heart's desire, and Dorothy and Toto find themselves safely back home in Kansas.

The Authors

Music and Lyrics by Harold Arlen and E.Y. Harburg; Background Music by Herbert Stothart; Adapted from the film by John Kane for the Royal Shakespeare Company (RSC). Based upon the Classical Motion Picture owned by Turner Entertainment Co. and distributed in all media by Warner Bros. Note: there is a second adaptation available for stage production with book adaptations by Frank Gabrielson. This version was originally produced by the Municipal Theatre of St. Louis (the MUNY) in 1945.

New York Run

There have been no Broadway or Off-Broadway productions of either the RSC or MUNY versions of this musical.

The Song

"Over the Rainbow"

At the beginning of the story, we see Dorothy on the farm, trying to get the grown-ups around her to hear what she has to say about mean neighbor Miss Gulch . But all of them are too busy trying to get their work done, and Aunt Em advises Dorothy, "Find a place where you won't get into any trouble." Alone with Toto, Dorothy dreams of just such a place in "Over the Rainbow."

Song Type

Standard Ballad/Tin Pan Alley Standard/Judy Garland signature song

Suggested 16-Bar Cut for Auditions

m. 49 to the end (m. 66). This is 18 bars, which

is generally acceptable for a 16-bar audition. If you prefer not to use the piano interlude (m. 57-m. 60), you could cut these measures, and sing the "If" (as written in m. 60) on the "and of 4" in measure 56.

Working

The Show

Based on Studs Terkel's nonfiction book of interviews with real people, *Working* explores the everyday lives of a wide variety of American workers, how they feel about their jobs, and how their jobs define who they are. In the course of the play, twenty-six workers--from newsboy to corporate executive—use songs and monologues to describe their daily routines and to express their hopes and dreams for the future.

The Authors

Original songs with Music and Lyrics by Craig Carnelia, Micki Grant, Mary Rodgers, Stephen Schwartz and James Taylor; Additional Spanish Lyrics by Graciela Danielle and Matt Landers; Book adapted by Stephen Schwartz and Nina Faso from the book by Studs Terkel. The song "Millwork" was written by James Taylor.

New York Run

May 14–June 4, 1978 at the 46th Street Theatre. The role of Grace Clements was originated by Bobo Lewis.

The Song

"Millwork"

In the song "Millwork," Grace sings about the relentless boredom and monotony of her factory job, and her regret and anger at having wasted her youth and life.

Song Type

Contemporary Musical Theater Ballad (Folk)

Suggested 16-Bar Cut for Auditions

m. 113 (including pick-up) through m. 130, then use m. 143 & m. 144 to finish out the song. This is 20 bars total, which is generally acceptable for a 16-bar audition.

PLOT SYNOPSES AND COMMENTARY BY
JOHN L. HAAG AND JEREMY MANN

The Songs

MY OWN BEST FRIEND

(from "Chicago")

Words by
FRED EBB

Music by
JOHN KANDER

One thing I know and I've al-ways known

I am my own best friend

ba-by's a-live but ba-by's a-lone and

BACK ON BASE
(from "Closer Than Ever")

Words by
RICHARD MALTBY, Jr.

Music by
DAVID SHIRE

in - spi - ra - tion___ Now I'm back on___ base.___

My ba - by plays a line that's___ sub - tle,___

(*mp*)

Yet___ it makes___ the strong - est___ case.___ An ar - gu - ment with

no re - but - tal___ Got me back on___ base.___

* Throughout, parts in cue-sized notes are merely a suggestion, and performers are encouraged to make the ad lib. scat sections "their own."

THAT MISTER MAN OF MINE

(from "Dames At Sea")

Words and Music by
JIM WISE, ROBIN MILLER
and GEORGE HAIMSOHN,

No king or tsar no Demp-sey or Gene Tun-ney

no mo-vie star his face was kind of fun-ny no Loch-in-var but

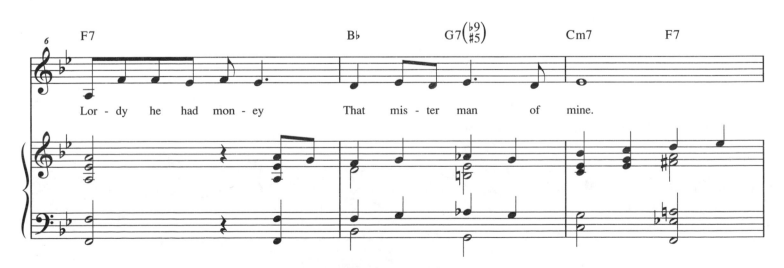

Lor-dy he had mon-ey That mis-ter man of mine.

38

That Mister Man Of Mine - 7 - 2
29007

gone's my de-sire now he's on re-lief That mis-ter man of

mine.

"Oh, Dick, it's divine, it gets you right here, and it'll be perfect for my first act closer."

No king or tsar no Demp-sey or Gene Tun-ney

no mo-vie star his face was kind of fun-ny no Loch-in-var but

A LITTLE BRAINS, A LITTLE TALENT

(from "Damn Yankees")

Words and Music by
RICHARD ADLER and JERRY ROSS

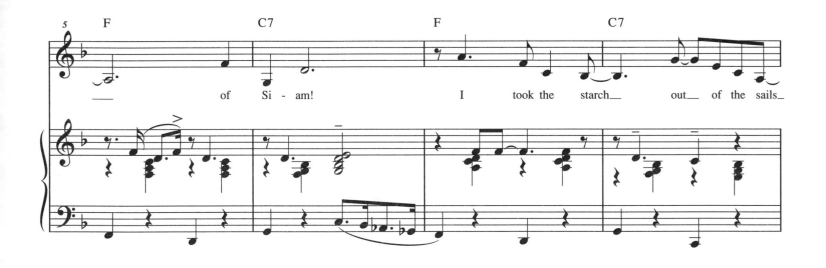

A Little Brains, A Little Talent - 8 - 4
29007

48

SOMETHING OF MY OWN

(from "Dessa Rose")

Lyrics by
LYNN AHRENS

Music by
STEPHEN FLAHERTY

LADIES
(from "Destry Rides Again")

Words and Music by
HAROLD ROME and GERRY ALSEN

I KNOW THE TRUTH

(from Elton John and Tim Rice's "Aida")

Lyrics by
TIM RICE

Music by
ELTON JOHN

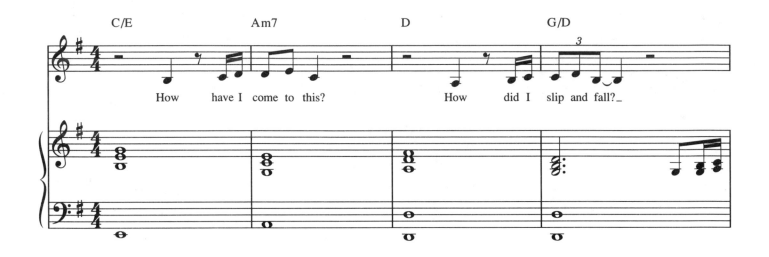

How have I come to this? How did I slip and fall?

How did I throw half a life-time a-way_____ with-out an-y thought at all?

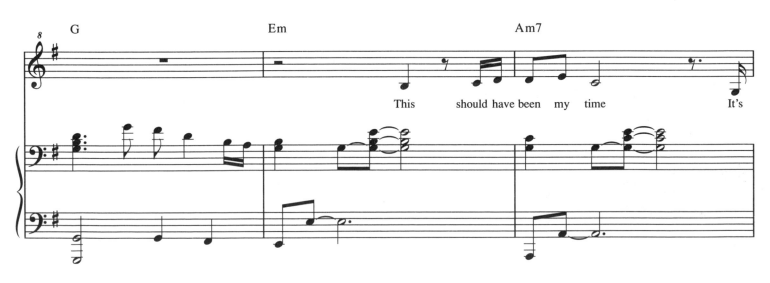

This should have been my time It's

HOLDING TO THE GROUND

(from "Falsettos")

Words and Music by
WILLIAM FINN

Flowingly, in 2

I was sure grow-ing up I would live the life__ my mo-ther as-sumed__ I'd live. Ve-ry Jew-ish ve-ry mid-dle class. And ve-ry__ straight. Where heal-thy men__ stayed

THINK OF MERYL STREEP

(from "Fame—The Musical")

Lyrics by
STEVE MARGOSHES

Music by
JACQUES LEVY

think of Ger-ry Page, think of all the feel - ings___
wast - ed on this creep,
think how you could use them,___ think of Mer - yl
Streep!

A LITTLE GIRL FROM LITTLE ROCK

(from "Gentlemen Prefer Blondes")

Lyrics by
LEO ROBIN

Music by
JULE STYNE

LAZY AFTERNOON

(from "The Golden Apple")

Words by
JOHN LaTOUCHE

Music by
JEROME MOROSS

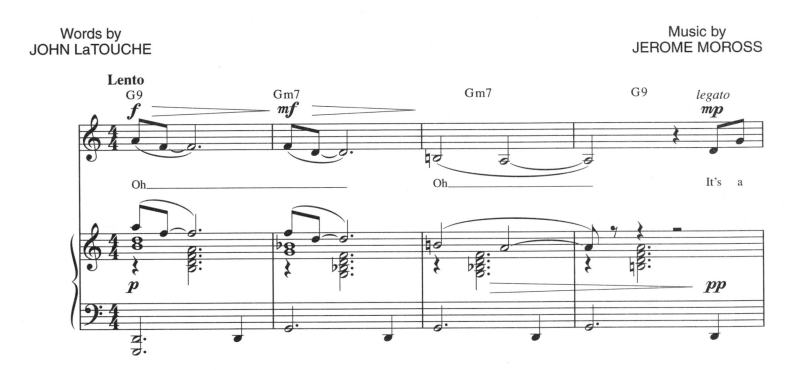

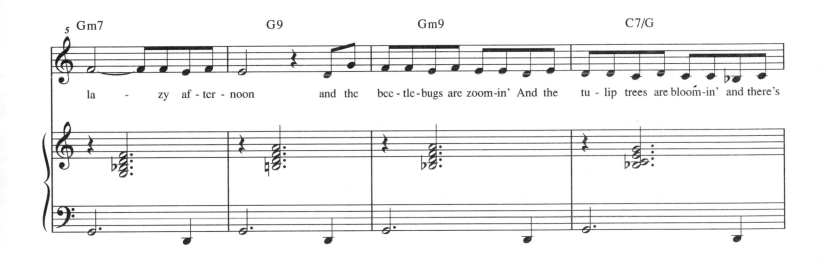

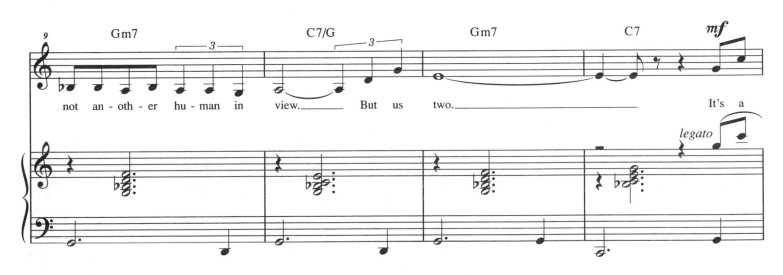

Lazy Afternoon - 4 - 1
29007

WHAT IS A WOMAN?

(from "I Do, I Do")

Words by
TOM JONES

Music by
HARVEY SCHMIDT

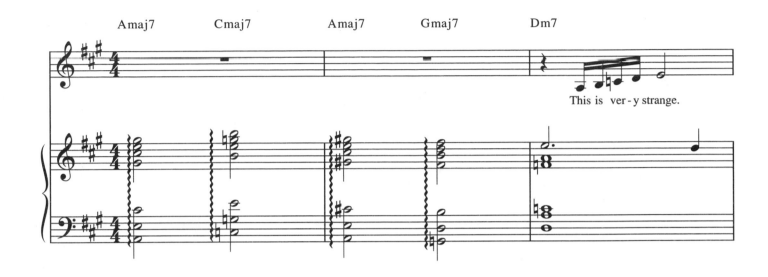

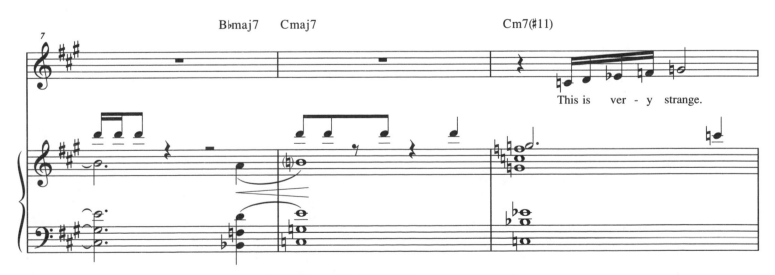

What Is A Woman? - 5 - 1
29007

OLD FRIEND

(from "I'm Getting My Act Together and Taking It On The Road")

Lyrics by
GRETCHEN CRYER

Music by
NANCY FORD

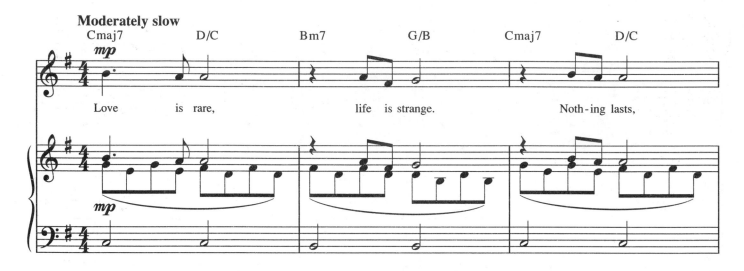

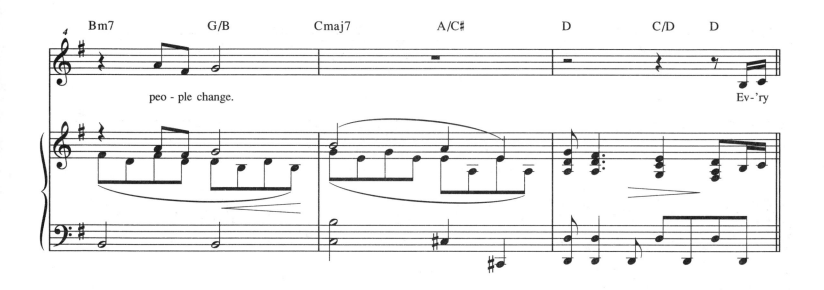

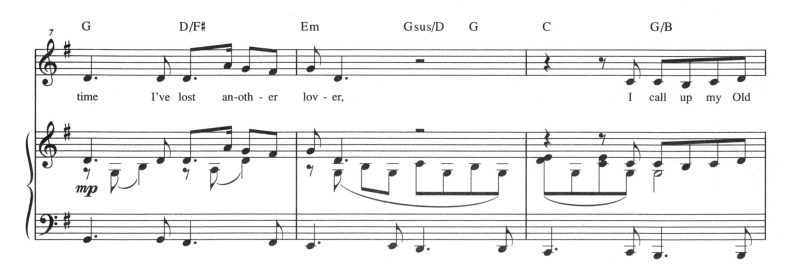

MOMENTS IN THE WOODS

(from "Into The Woods")

Music and Lyrics by
STEPHEN SONDHEIM

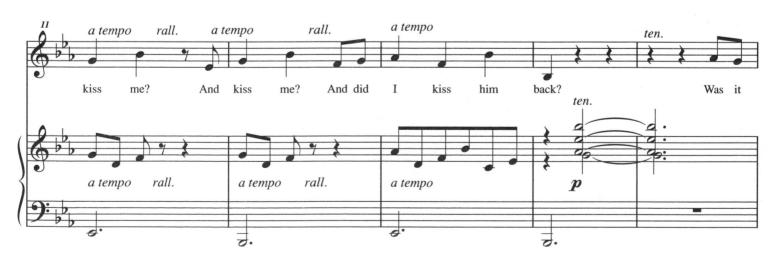

Last Midnight
(from the musical "Into the Woods")

Music and Lyrics by
STEPHEN SONDHEIM

Allegretto (♩ = 152)

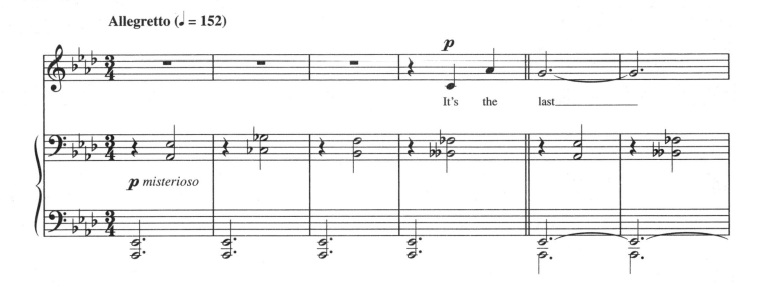

It's the last _____

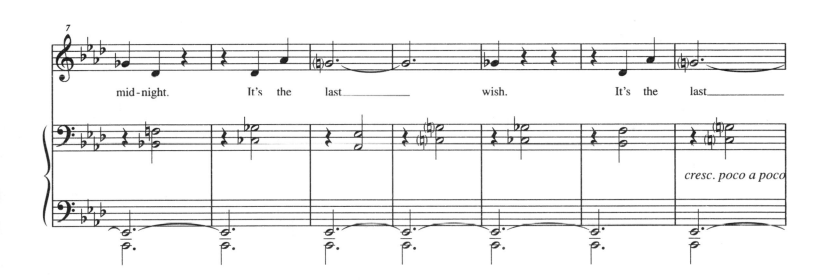

mid-night. It's the last _____ wish. It's the last _____

_____ mid-night, Soon it will be Boom _____ Squish!

(Stamps her foot) (Squish sound)

good, I'm not nice, I'm just right. I'm the Witch. You're the world. I'm the hitch, I'm what no one be - lieves, I'm the Witch. You're all li - ars and thieves, Like his fa - ther, Like his son will be,

verse. Now, be-fore it's past_____ mid - night,_____

_____ I'm leav-ing you my last_____ curse:

I'm leav-ing you a - lone. You can tend the gar - den, it's yours._____

_____ Sep-'rate and a - lone, Ev -'ry-bod - y down on all fours._____ All right, Moth - er,

SOMEWHERE THAT'S GREEN
(from "Little Shop Of Horrors")

Lyrics by
HOWARD ASHMAN

Music by
ALAN MENKIN

Tempo Ad lib.

I know Sey-mour's the great-est but I'm da-ting a

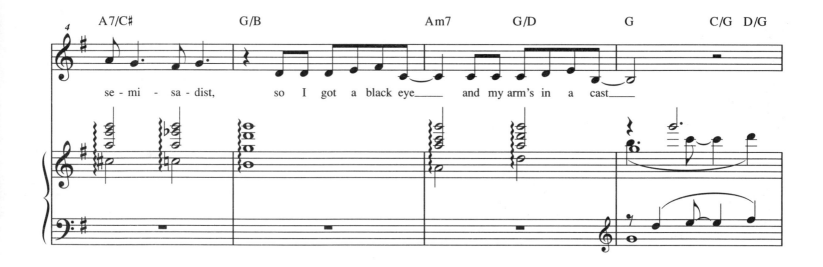

se-mi-sa-dist, so I got a black eye and my arm's in a cast

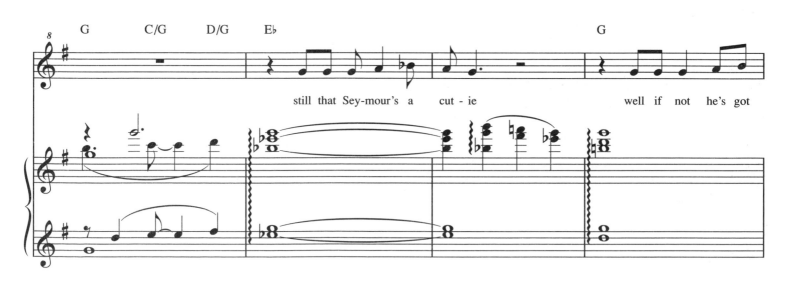

still that Sey-mour's a cut-ie well if not he's got

WEST END AVENUE

(from "The Magic Show")

Words and Music by
STEPHEN SCHWARTZ

You win a - gain!

TELL ME WHY
(from "A Man Of No Importance")

Lyrics by
LYNN AHRENS

Music by
STEPHEN FLAHERTY

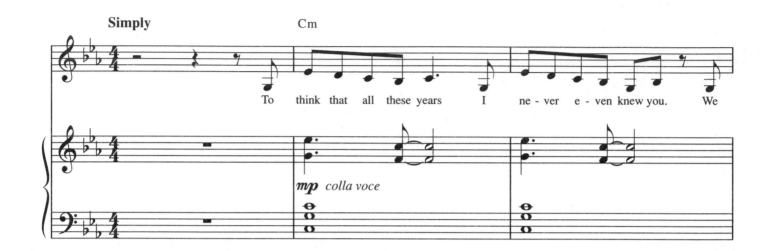

To think that all these years I ne-ver e-ven knew you. We

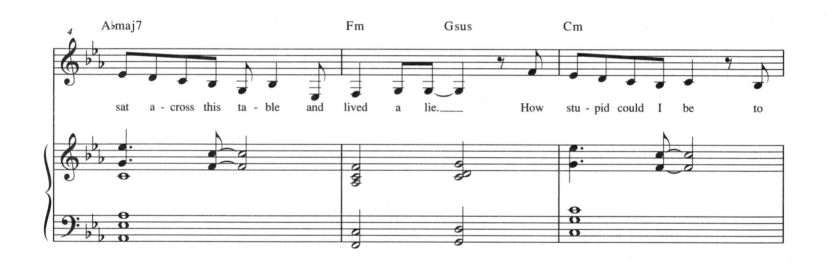

sat a-cross this ta-ble and lived a lie.___ How stu-pid could I be to

look but ne-ver see! Now tell me why___ I was-ted half my life and

TAKE IT ON THE CHIN
(from "Me And My Girl")

Words by
ARTHUR ROSE and
DOUGLAS FURBER

Music by
NOEL GAY

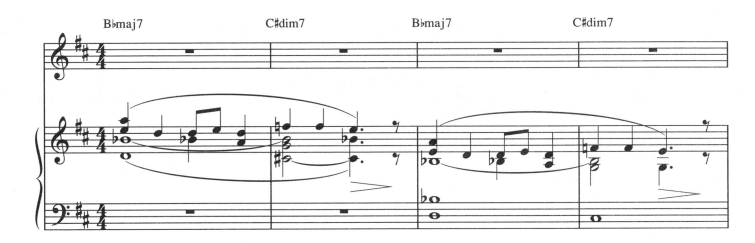

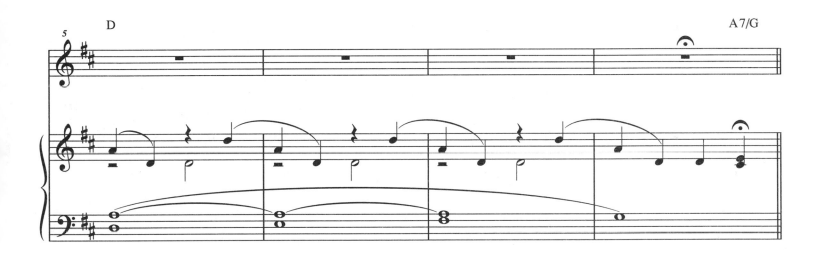

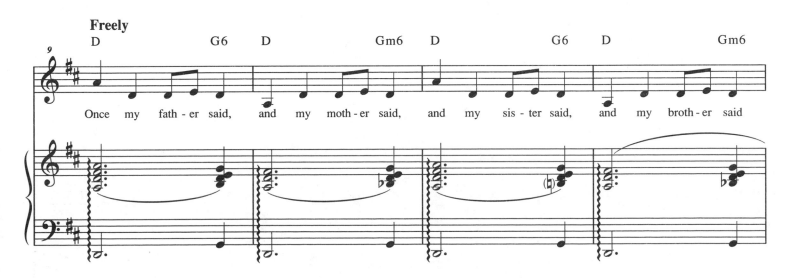

Once my fath-er said, and my moth-er said, and my sis-ter said, and my broth-er said

136

LIKE IT WAS

(from "Merrily We Roll Along")

Music and Lyrics by
STEPHEN SONDHEIM

Blames the way it is   On___ the way it

was.   On the way it nev - er

ev - er   was.

THE MUSIC STILL PLAYS ON

(from "A New Brain")

Words and Music by
WILLIAM FINN

The Music Still Plays On - 8 - 1
29007

MAD ABOUT THE BOY

(from "Words And Music")

Words and Music by
NOEL COWARD

IT'S A FINE LIFE

from "Oliver!"

Words and Music by
LIONEL BART

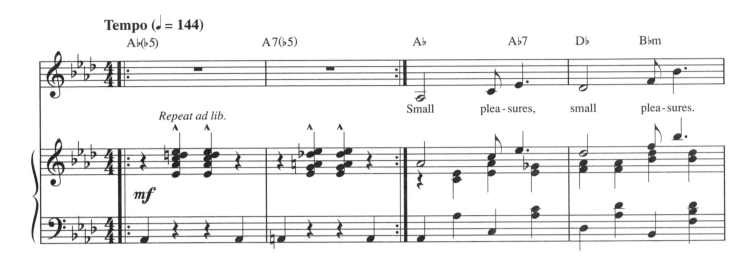

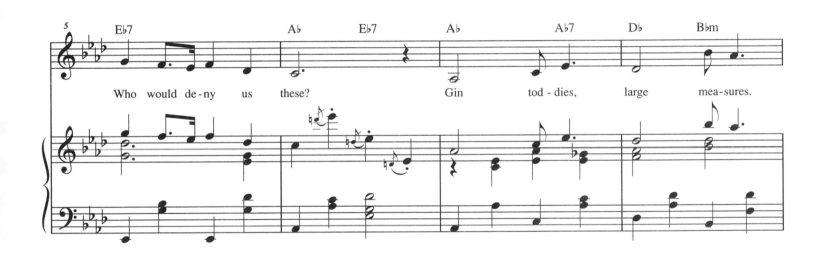

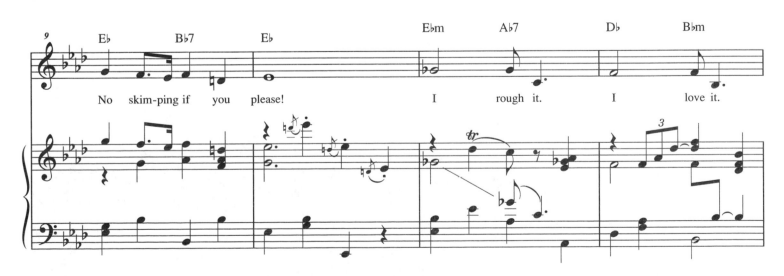

HOW CAN I WAIT?
(from "Paint Your Wagon")

Lyrics by
ALAN JAY LERNER

Music by
FREDERICK LOEWE

ZIP

(from "Pal Joey")

Words by
LORENZ HART

Music by
RICHARD RODGERS

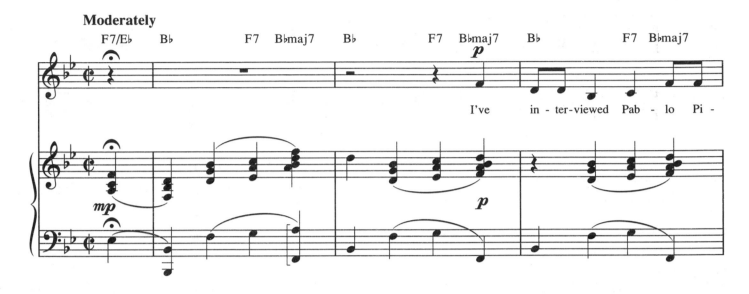

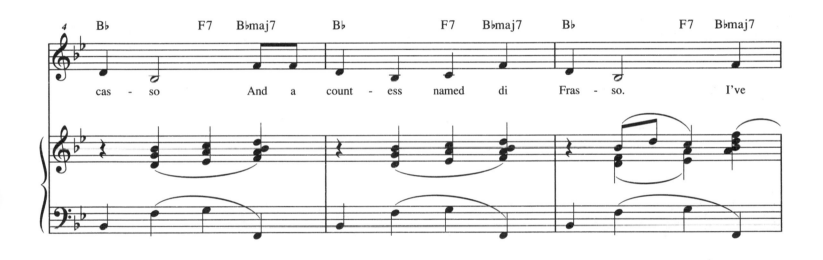

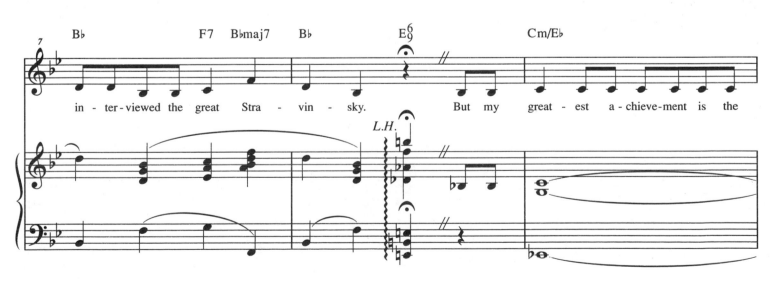

Zip - 5 - 1
29007

I don't like a deep con-tral-to, Or a man who's voice is al-to.
I don't care for Whist-ler's moth-er, Char-lie's aunt, or Shu-bert's bro-ther.
I don't care for ei-ther Mick-ey — Mouse and Roon-ey make me sick-y!

Zip! I'm a het-er-o-sex-ual. Zip! It took in-tel-lect to
Zip! I'm mis-o-gyn-is-tic. Zip! My in-tel-li-gence is
Zip! I'm a lit-tle hec-tic. Zip! My ar-tis-tic taste is

mas-ter my art. _____ Zip! Who the hell is Mar-gie
guid-ing my hand. _____ Zip! Who the hell is Sal-ly
clas-sic and dear. _____ Zip! Who the hell is Li-li St.

Hart? _____
Rand? _____

Cyr? _____

MY COUSIN IN MILWAUKEE

(from "Pardon My English")

Music and Lyrics by
GEORGE GERSHWIN
and IRA GERSHWIN

Molto moderato

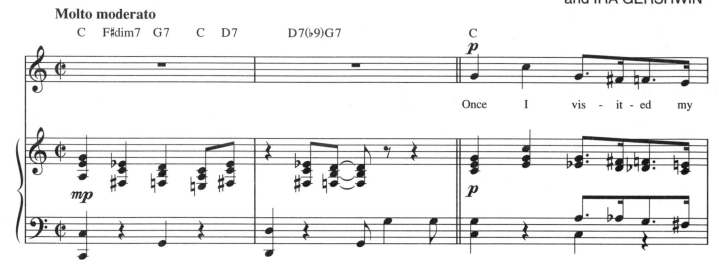

Once I vis-it-ed my

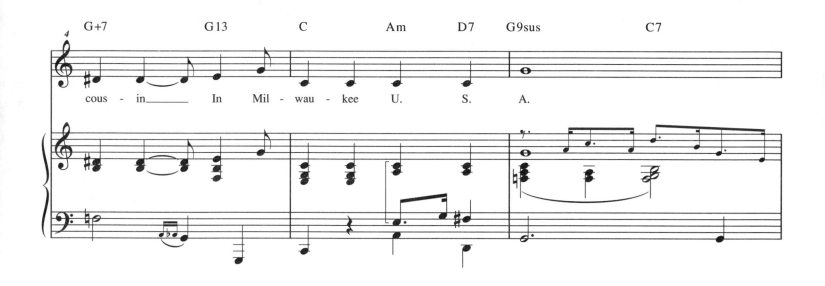

cous-in_____ In Mil-wau-kee U. S. A.

She got boy-friends by the doz-en_____ When she sang in a low-down

My Cousin In Milwaukee - 7 - 1
29007

NOTICE ME, HORTON

(from "Seussical")

Words by
LYNN AHRENS

Music by
STEPHEN FLAHERTY

WONDERFUL, WONDERFUL DAY

(from "Seven Brides For Seven Brothers")

Words and Music by
JOHNNY MERCER and GENE DePAUL

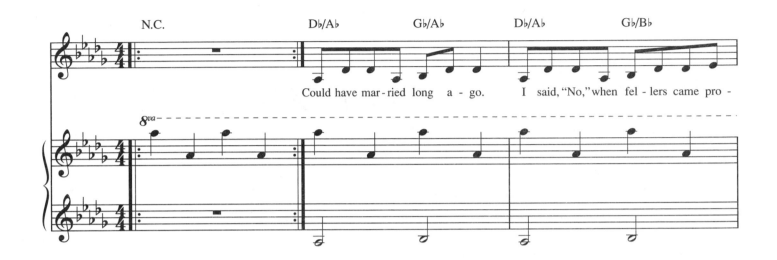

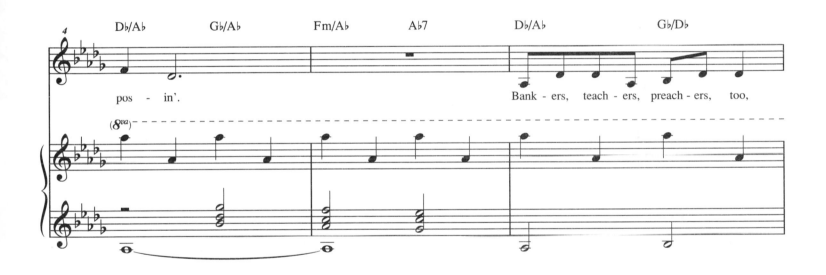

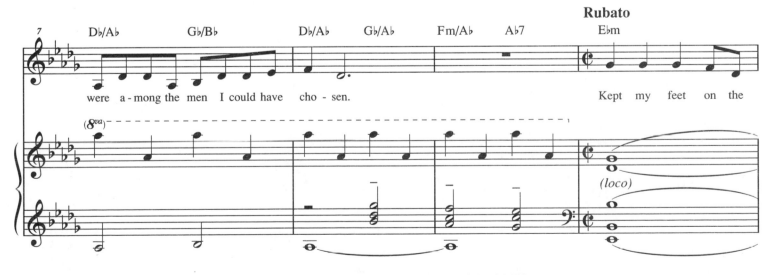

194

WHAT A NICE IDEA
(from "Two Gentlemen Of Verona")

Lyrics by
JOHN GUARE

Music by
GALT MacDERMONT

Be-cause he loves her, He de-spis-es me. Be-cause I

love him, I pit-y him. If I could be her

just for a mo-ment, When he was hold-ing her I would in-

What A Nice Idea - 5 - 1
29007

IF YOU HADN'T BUT YOU DID

(from "Two On The Aisle")

Lyrics by
BETTY COMDEN and
ADOLPH GREEN

Music by
JULE STYNE

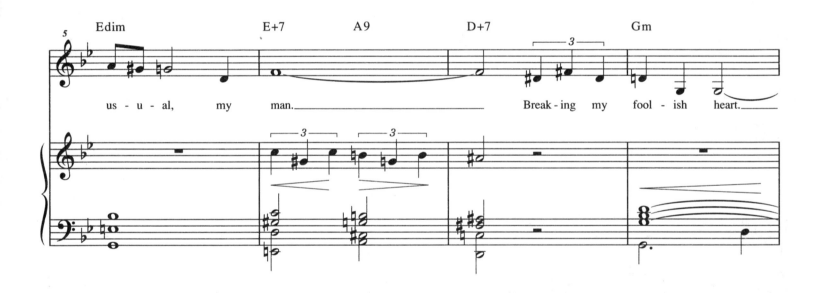

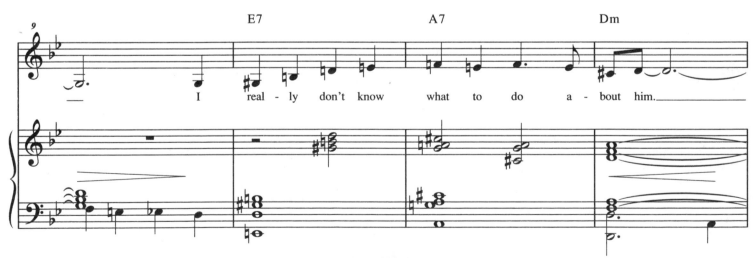

OVER THE RAINBOW
(from "The Wizard of Oz")

Lyric by
E. Y. HARBURG

Music by
HAROLD ARLEN

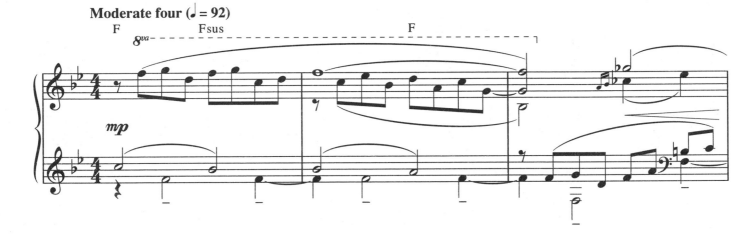

When all the world is a hope-less jum-ble, And the

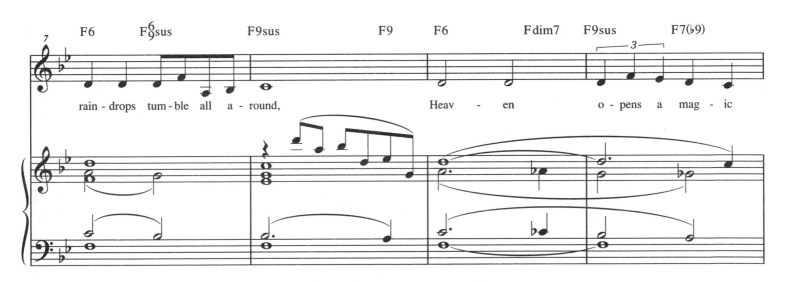

rain-drops tum-ble all a-round, Heav - en o - pens a mag - ic

MILLWORK
from "Working"

Words and Music by
JAMES TAYLOR

My mind be-gins to wan - der to my days back on___ the farm,___ and I can___

and the rest of my life.